unsent texts

Sarah Cole

BookLeaf Publishing

India | USA | UK

Presentation by *BookLeaf Publishing*

Web: www.bookleafpub.com

E-mail: info@bookleafpub.com

ISBN: 9789363313262

First edition 2024

To, you

Love, me

ACKNOWLEDGEMENT

To my lifelong best friend: Thank you, Kristi, for being a source of encouragement and loving me through all my phases in life. You are the living proof that soulmates come in the form of friends, too.

I also can't thank my mom enough for giving me the gift of creativity and continuously reminding me to lean into it. You taught me how to look for the beautiful but often missed moments in life. You provided a priceless example of leading a life of gratitude. I love you.

PREFACE

These poems are built from scattered thoughts, unsent texts, and late night musings. In 2023, I began to write notes filled with them. I didn't quite know how to organize them. When I was given the chance to publish, I had to take it and complete this writing journey.

As you read from beginning to end, you see the creation of something beautiful. The forming of love. The further you get into the book, you will begin experiencing the chronological breakdown of this love and the eventual acceptance of what it has become.

I wrote this to navigate and to honor the journey. Despite the ending, I would retake this path over and over just to live it again.

the start

I was once told that the true definition of love is
caring for someone so intensely that you
prioritize their well-being.
When we met, I could feel the selflessness
creeping in.
Knocking on the door of my heart that I had
locked up so carefully.

I was ready to open it up and give you a spare
key.
Step inside.
I'm ready to love and be loved.
Are you?

Walk around my soul and make yourself
comfortable.
Enjoy the delicately placed memories pinned to
the walls.
It was as if I had already memorized all the
details of your spirit,
Falling in love with each imperfection.

I had seen a million different faces.
But none felt like home quite like you.

bubble

I couldn't possibly realize
The ability we have
A strength of this size

Creating a bubble so pure and clean
No one can get inside
Time stopped, it seemed

He leans in to laugh while we sit protected
Not knowing the world continues
We're simply undetected

No matter the trouble, the stress, or pain
We didn't feel anything in this space
We created this domain

The joy I felt watching him glow
Knowing he felt it, too
When our bubble began to grow

This bubble meant safety, love, and respect
We had so much fun
Our hearts did connect

Each time we got together, we stepped back
inside
No room for any bad
Removing all pride

No harm is brought from outside this bubble
We'd keep us safe
We swore to each other, regardless of trouble

your love feels like

One day, you will meet someone who turns
everything around
The entire world becomes deja vu
Because none of the universe is unfamiliar
anymore

You see them in your daily tasks
In these small moments, you know they'd love
'I wish they were here,' you think

They feel like a nap on a lazy day
Warmed by the sun
Hugged by your favorite blanket

It feels like their fingers ran through
Every knot of your soul
Smoothing them over so gently

You share all your past experiences
To catch them up on your life
Preparing for every future encounter to include
them

The halls of your shared space are filled with
laughter

Knowing exactly what jokes the other loves
Developing a new, unspoken language in the
process

They feel like a late-night visit to the kitchen
Silently sharing a favorite dish
They always give you the last bite

One day, you will meet someone who turns
everything around

best friend

"So this is what it feels like to be in love with your best friend?"

clock

"I wish we could make time stop."
I say,
As I stare at the clock

"I wish we could make time stop"
He said,
As he pulls the batteries out of the clock.

umbrella

You came into my life like a sunny day.
Sweeping me off my feet.
I fell more in love with you
Every time that we would speak.

I noticed as our time went on
That storms become more present.
So I held onto you - my umbrella
To make it a bit more pleasant.

I closed my eyes and trusted
That you would keep me dry.
I held on tight and still felt rain
I began to cry.

My tears ran down my cheeks.
As I slowly realized
It wasn't just rain that fell
But water from my eyes.

I pried them open to look around
And broke my heart as I looked up
The umbrella - you- meant to keep me dry
Is where the storm came from

The only way to step outside
From the waters where I drown.
Is to unclench my fingers one by one
And finally, set you down.

grief

I'm grieving you while we hold hands.

I silently say goodbye to the plans we made
Fold up the blueprints of our dream home to
tuck away

I'm grieving you while we kiss.

Knowing your lips will connect with another's
Closing my eyes while you place my hair behind
my ear

I'm grieving you while we laugh.

The inside jokes opening doors to the public
Feeling my smile drift away

I'm grieving you while you stand next to me.
Not knowing when the last time will be.

Let me grieve just a little longer.

did you know?

"I thought you were my soulmate.

My love had developed so deeply and intensely that I was sure of it. I was sure we'd be together forever.

This burning feeling is part of us up in flames. Some of my favorite parts."

timelines

I see you in every timeline
We are happy in some
In others, we are not

In many, we never truly meet
Except for a casual passing
Just a shared space in a line

I see you in every timeline
Succeeding with me by your side
Content with our lives and fulfilled

Others are filled with a desire
To always find something bigger and better
We build resentment because of this

I see you in every timeline
Watching our lives intertwine
Flowing in and out of infinite possibilities

I wonder which we're in now
How will this end, and will we be happy
Do you think there is a way to choose

I see you in every timeline.

dream

"I sleep so that we can meet."

my temple

I created wall after wall
Creating beautiful layers
Heavily locked and increasingly tall

My soul is at the center of it
No windows
Just a single door to it

You made it through each pleat of my protection
Banging at the door
Rummaging and tossing, looking for some
direction

You pulled down the wallpaper
The fabrics of my being, asking,
Was it authentic - or was I a faker

You preferred something to your own taste
Crown molding it to your liking
All the work I had done going to waste

alchemized anger

In my heart, in veins of blue,
A chemistry stirs, my soul does brew.
Anger, a strong and ruthless ride,
From a single spark to a raging tide.

It starts as whispers, then it swells,
Within me is where it dwells.
My body shakes, my pulse begins to race
Tears start to run down my face.

My muscles tense, fists clenched tight,
As anger peaks, it consumes my night.
Inside my heart, where it roams,
A chemical storm finds its home.

But like all things, it ebbs away,
Leaving echoes of its stay.
In human form, a crucible deep,
Where anger stirs, and secrets keep.

don't reply

"I want you to know I miss you. No additional context. No guilt. No anger. No expectation that you'll fix this.

I don't want you to feel bad or tell me it'll get better.

This is where we are meant to be - apart from each other. A little empty. A little sad."

the apologies you didn't want

I'm sorry that I never said sorry in the ways you needed.

I am sorry that I overwhelmed you.

There were times when I felt so alone with my thoughts that I didn't know what to do. I'm sorry.

I am scared that I'm not enough and too much at once. I'm too emotional, too weak, not stable enough, and not good enough. I'm sorry for my insecurities.

When I feel your hot and cold demeanor, my mind goes into hyperdrive. I'm sorry. I don't want to do that.

I'm sorry I failed to give you what you had asked for.

These aren't the apologies you'd hoped for. I'm sorry

        I'm sorry, but can you hold my hand?

giving it back

I open a box and find all the pieces to lay out
and see
I count them as I slowly come to terms with
reality

I note the memories of us, piling them up tall
Stacking higher and higher, praying they won't
fall

Over here are the kisses, the touches, and the sex
And over there, are even more unforgettable
objects

I fold up these details so very nice and clean
I ignore the little voice inside wanting to scream

Pushing that aside, I wrap twine around our
plans
Looking past the fact we never made it to France

Let me not forget the dried flowers
Or the shared showers
Not even the long talks after hours

I'll place those neatly inside, too

I roll up the blanket of passion that covered our
bodies
I place it next to the endless hours of shared
hobbies

I can't leave out the silent moments, either
Resetting and holding each other for a breather

Those get placed right next to the laughs
But not to be overshadowed but the bubble baths

Telling me stories of your childhood
Gets arranged precisely next to my motherhood

The box fills up faster than I could have thought
I stand back and realize there's not one empty
spot

So I'll close it up softly then give it a kiss
And maybe one day you'll open to reminisce

final act of love

I used to want things I did for you to be special

Unique in some way

I imagined giving you a love you had never
experienced before

But I know now my love for you surpasses my
desire to be special

I pray you continue to be loved the way I love
you - and then some

May your car rides home always be filled with a
voice that brings a smile to your face

I hope your bedtimes are completed with held
hands and shared dreams

I hope your movies are paused frequently for
new predictions and discussions

And that your room is filled with blue lights and
stars

I picture your future with satisfied FOMO and
train rides to the edge of plans

I hope the hurt I brought you is dissipated by the
overwhelming feeling of contentment

And your disappointment fades through the
years with the help of met expectations

I pray your future love gives you all the love I
gave - and then some.

For one day, you will see that my final act of
love
Is loving you in silence while you live your life
without me.

disappearing text

The chime of my phone startles me
I open it to your name further down the list of
texts

At first, you sat safely atop
Pinned and secured

But eventually, your name brought sadness
So, I had to create some space between you and
reality

Slowly but surely, your name became lower
                and lower
and lower

I revisit it often
Kind of like an old friend

I pretend it's a love letter you left behind for me
As I scan the texts - just in case I missed
something

I'm careful not to touch anything, though
I don't want to accidentally send "i miss you"

something stupid

"I miss you"

Sent.